Mel Bay's First Lessons™

Flatpicking Guitar

by Joe Carr

1 2 3 4 5 6 7 8 9 0

It doesn't get any easier.....

Visit us on the Web at www.melbay.com — E-mail us at email@melbay.com

Table of Contents

Flatpicking guitar by Joe Carr

Lightening fast runs, hot licks, and fiddle tunes are all part of the exciting style of guitar playing called Flatpicking. Although many styles feature the use of the plectrum or flatpick, the term "flatpicking" is commonly used to refer to country, folk or bluegrass style picking on an acoustic guitar.

Players such as Doc Watson, Norman Blake, Tony Rice and Clarence White popularized this great style which is now heard at jam sessions everywhere.

Although flatpicking is also used to solo on singing songs, we will concentrate here on instrumental music. American fiddle tunes were the inspiration for much of modern flatpicking and learning fiddle tunes is still the quickest and most fun way to develop good pick control and an understanding of scales and how they lay out on the fingerboard.

About the Author

Guitar players may not recognize Joe Carr's name, but his face is probably familiar. He appears in over twenty instructional guitar videos ranging from country to western swing, bluegrass and even heavy metal! Add to these his videos on mandolin, fiddle, banjo and ukulele and Joe may be the most recorded video instructor anywhere.

Joe is a self-taught musician who started guitar at age 13. After six years touring with Alan Munde in the internationally acclaimed bluegrass group COUNTRY GAZETTE, Joe left to join the music faculty in the unique commercial music program at South Plains College in Levelland, Texas.

Today, in addition to teaching, Joe continues to perform in a duo setting with former employer and South Plains College colleague, Alan Munde. Alan and Joe have recorded three CD's under their names and completed an award-winning book on West Texas country music in 1995.

Equipment

The country flatpick technique was developed primarily on flattop acoustic guitars. Early flatpickers developed a unique sound using open strings in their chords and licks. This works particularly well in the keys of G, C, E, D, and A. To play in keys such as B, B♭, and F, flatpickers typically use a capo to allow the use of more familiar positions. This practice also provides the characteristic open-string sound in non-open keys. For example, to play in B, many players capo at the fourth fret and play in the G position. The chart below explains other applications.

Capos

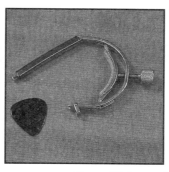

When buying a capo, look for one that is adjustable. Spring and elastic capos can be difficult to use and the tension may be too strong or weak for your particular guitar neck. Capos that adjust with a screw mechanism can be set with just the right tension to fret the strings without buzzing and without any tuning distortion. Place the capo close to, but not on top of the fret. Some guitars may require some slight retuning after the capo is in place, but before going to this extreme, try pulling any sharp strings slightly. Sometimes this will take the slack out of the string and return it to correct pitch. Any tuning you do with the capo on will affect the open tuning, presuming you tuned without out a capo first. This could put you out of tune with other instruments in an ensemble. There will be more on this in the tuning section. Players usually only capo as high as the fifth fret, unless there is another guitar player playing in a lower position or for special effects.

Straps

If you plan to stand while performing, you will need a strap. Leather or nylon will not harm the finish on your guitar as will some plastics. Most guitars come with an endpin for attaching a strap. There may or may not be a strap button on the heel of the neck to attach the other end of the strap. Although some straps are designed to be tied to the headstock of the guitar, most players opt to have a strap button placed on the lower side of the heel, close to the body, leaving room enough to attach the strap. Have a competent repair person do this work. Be sure the button is not placed too close to the fingerboard where it could interfere with left hand fingering up the neck.

Strings

Acoustic guitars generally sound best with bronze wrapped strings. The first and second strings will be plain and unwrapped steel, while the third through sixth strings will have a plain steel core wire wrapped with bronze wire. Many flatpickers use a standard medium set which measures; 0.13, 0.17, 0.26, 0.36, 0.46, and 0.56. If you find this set too hard to play, you could use a medium light set with an 0.11 or 0.12 first string. Do not use an unwound third string as this produces a thin "tinny" sound. Various alloys are available, each with subtle differences in tone. Buy the cheapest name brand string set at first and experiment later, when your ear for string tone has developed. Most manufacturers make good strings these days, so it's actually hard to find "bad" strings.

Wipe your strings clean after you play. Dirt and moisture are the greatest killer of strings. If you have dry hands and wipe your strings regularly, you may go several months between string changes. If you have sweaty hands or live in a humid climate, you may have to change more often.

In any case, change the whole set anytime you break a string. If you are breaking a lot of strings, take your instrument to a repair person for adjustment. Excessive tuning problems and a dull, dead sound are other signs of worn out strings.

If you play a lot, your frets will eventually need attention. When you can see dents in the tops of the frets, it's time to visit the repair shop. A fret dressing (also called a fret mill or fret level) will re-level all the frets and make the guitar easier to play buzz-free. This operation can extend the life of your frets and put off the need for a fret job, which involves removal and replacement of individual frets. This work is considerably expensive, but necessary.

Tuning

The best guitarist in the world would sound terrible if the guitar is out of tune. Even beginners have control over this area of music making, so be very picky about it. Every time you play, take time to get your instrument in tune. Electronic tuners make this an easier job. Realize that while tuners try to tune your guitar perfectly, guitars are not perfect instruments. Each guitar has its own tuning idiosyncrasies that you will learn over time with careful observation. Perhaps you will have to tune one string slightly flat to the tuner in order to get it to sound good in a chord. Tuning is even more important when playing with other musicians.

Capo Chart

Use this chart to determine which chords to use when employing the capo. Notice there are several options available for each key.

Desired Key	Capo set at	Play in
B♭	1st fret	A
B♭	3rd fret	G
B	2nd fret	A
B	4th fret	G
C	5th fret	G
C	open - no capo	
C♯/D♭	1st fret	C
C♯/D♭	4th fret	A
D	2nd fret	C
D	open - no capo	
D♯/E♭	1st fret	D
D♯/E♭	3rd fret	C
E	open - no capo	
E	2nd fret	D

Desired Key	Capo set at	Play in
E	4th fret	C
F	1st fret	E
F	3rd fret	D
F	5th fret	C
F♯/G♭	2nd fret	E
F♯/G♭	4th fret	D
G	open - no capo	
G	3rd fret	E
G	5th fret	D
G♯/A♭	1st fret	G
G♯/A♭	4th fret	E
A	2nd fret	G
A	5th fret	E
A	open - no capo	

Choosing a Flatpick

If you are a beginner, get a selection of flatpicks. The three cornered teardrop shape is very popular, but you can experiment with different shapes. For years, tortoiseshell was the pick material of choice and some players still use it. For legal, ecological and financial reasons, plastic picks are now the most common. There are many types of plastic and you should try them all. Pick selection is one of the most personal decisions you will make as a flatpicker. Picks are the least expensive accessory a guitarist uses, so buy lots of them and experiment.

Begin with at least a medium thickness pick. As your technique develops, you may move to a heavy or even extra-heavy. Heavier picks produce more volume, speed and better tone, but they are more difficult to control.

Holding the Pick

How you hold the pick is also an individual decision, but many people use some variation of the following method. Place the pick on the fleshy pad of your right thumb. Make sure it is not on the joint of the thumb. Place your index finger on the other side of the pick. With the guitar in normal playing position, place the pick against the sixth string. Your thumb should be parallel to the string while the index fingers points toward the guitar top. Although there are many variations, this is a great place to start.

Right Hand Position

While there are many variations, I will describe the method used by many top professionals and which is probably the most common successful approach. Be aware that no player picks the same way all the time. Certain techniques may demand different hand positions.

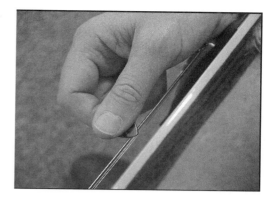

Start with the strap on the guitar (if you have one) and centered in your lap or slightly to the left, (maybe on your left thigh). Place your right hand wrist just above the bridge. Lower your hand until you feel the bridge pins (the plastic pins that keep the strings in the holes) lightly touching the bottom of your palm. Moving at the wrist, pick a string with a downstroke followed by an upstroke. Your pick holding fingers should remain still and just hold the pick. The other right hand fingers should be relaxed and not clenched into a fist. Let the movement come from the wrist and do not press onto the bridge.

Your right hand should not be planted in one place on the bridge. As you move from string to string, the right hand should drift across the tops of the bridge pins, allowing your wrist to center over the strings you are playing. Some players find it helpful to let the third and/or fourth fingers drag lightly on the pickguard as they pick. This can stabilize the right hand and act as a depth gauge. This approach is acceptable, as long as you don't anchor those fingers in place on the pickguard. Anchored fingers will stiffen your wrist - very undesirable!

Pick Direction

Pick direction, in my opinion, is the most important aspect of flatpicking. Most flatpickers use the technique called "alternating picking." This is the area where many beginning students have the most problems. If you are a beginner with no experience, simply follow the pick direction arrows carefully and you will soon develop a "feel" for correct alternating pick direction.

If you have played a little already, you may have developed a few bad habits. Unplanned consecutive down and upstrokes (I call this random picking) are not a problem at slow speeds, but can result in choppy playing at higher speeds. Breaking old habits is hard, but motivated students can standardize their picking in as little as two weeks of concentrated effort. It can be done and the benefits are many.

Basic Alternating Picking Rules

A measure of music in 4/4 time contains eight 8th notes. They can be counted "one and two and three and four and." Pick the third string (G) eight times starting with a downstroke and alternating strokes from there on. It looks like this in music and tablature. Notice downstrokes are indicated with this symbol (⊓), while upstrokes are indicated by (∨).

► EXERCISE ONE:

Repeat exercise 1, counting aloud. Notice that each downstroke is played as you say a number and each upstroke as you say "and."

What happens when there are not eight notes in a measure? Below is a measure of music with four beats. There are four quarter notes counted "ONE (and) TWO (and) THREE (and) FOUR (and).

► EXERCISE TWO:

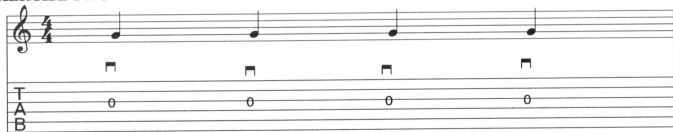

To play this measure, use all downstrokes since each quarter note last the time of two eight notes.

Here is a mixed measure of quarter and eight notes. We count this measure: "ONE, two and, THREE, four and." It is picked Down, Down-Up, Down, Down-Up.

► EXERCISE THREE:

If you have problems with this material, move on to the tune examples and follow the pick direction indicators. After you have played through a few songs it will make more sense.

Basic Chords

We will begin in the key of G. Here are the basic chords, also known as the 1, 4 and 5 chords, in G.

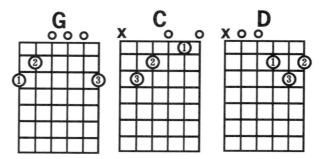

This is the basic strum pattern used by almost every flatpicker. It is called the Bass/Strum pattern.

▶ **EXERCISE FOUR:**

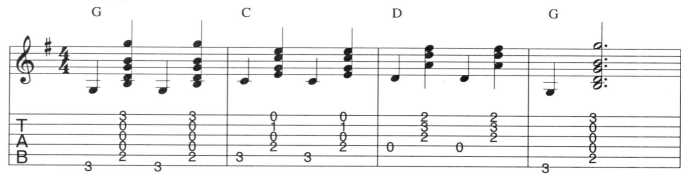

Here are the alternate bass notes for the G, C, and D chords.

▶ **EXERCISE FIVE:**

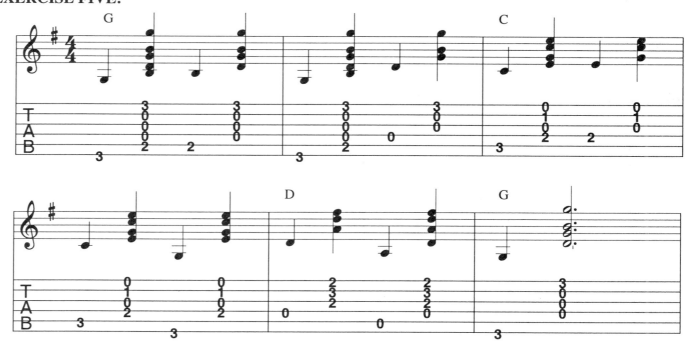

Try the alternating bass notes with strums in this exercise:

▶ **EXERCISE SIX:**

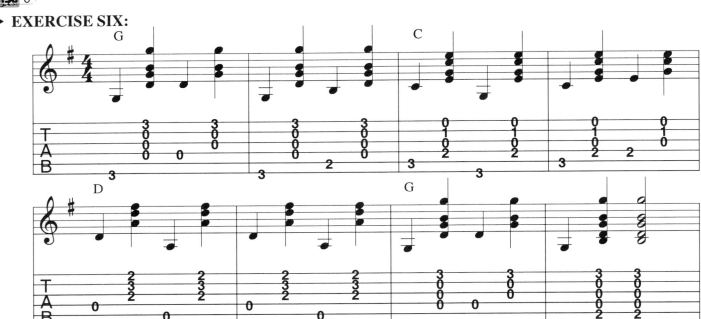

Here is a new bass pattern called the "walk-up." It can be reversed to produce a "walk-down."

▶ **EXERCISE SEVEN:**

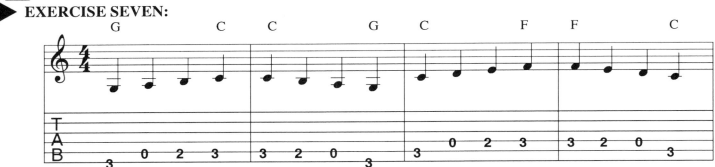

Practice this exercise which includes alternating bass, walk-ups and walk-downs.

▶ **EXERCISE EIGHT:**

Left Hand Techniques

Hammer-on

A hammer-on is a left hand technique that can add interest to your rhythm playing. To practice this technique, pick the low E string (sixth) with a downstroke. Quickly, and with force, fret the second fret of the sixth string with your left hand first finger. If you move too slowly, the string will be deadened. You must "hammer" your finger down onto the string so that it continues to ring. You want two distinct notes; the open E followed by the fretted F# at the second fret. Here is the exercise:

▶ **EXERCISE NINE:**

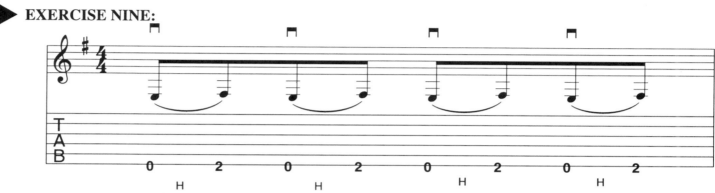

Now let's add the hammer-on to the basic strum pattern.

▶ **EXERCISE TEN:**

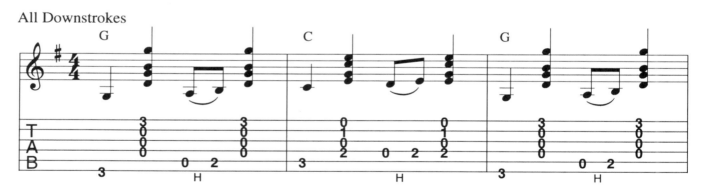

If the second note is muted, try using more force to hammer-on. Also try fretting with the hammer finger close to, but not on top of, the fret.

Pull-off

The pull-off is another left hand technique which is sort of a reverse hammer-on. Fret the second fret of the A string (fifth) with your first finger. Play the fretted B note with a downstroke and quickly pull the fingertip off the string causing the open A note to ring. If you lift your finger off the string, very little sound is produced. Remove your finger slightly to the side, so that you pluck the string as your finger leaves it. This technique is a case of: "If it hurts, you are probably doing it right!" Even if you have played guitar for quite a while, pull-offs will hurt until you have developed new "sideways" callouses.

▶ **EXERCISE ELEVEN:**

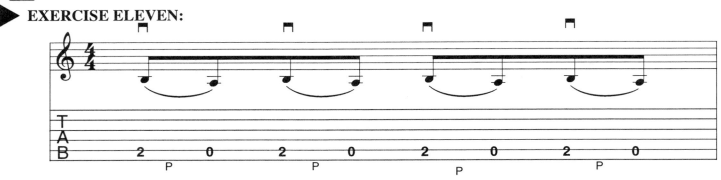

Bass-strum pull-off exercise

▶ **EXERCISE TWELVE:**

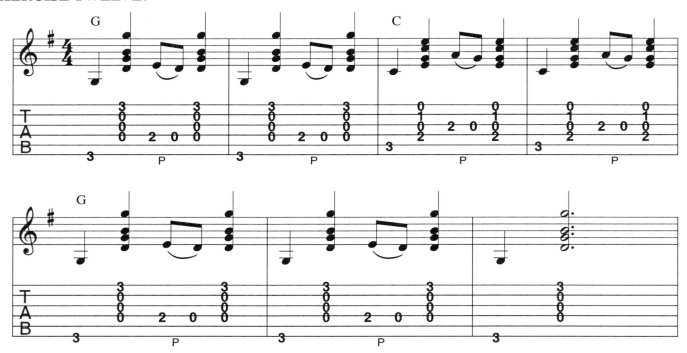

These two techniques may take lots of practice. Continue through these lessons and your left hand techniques will improve over time. Be aware that hammer-ons and pull-offs can be performed at any fret and with any finger or combination of fingers. The same is true for the third left hand effect: slides.

Slides

The slide is another left hand tool which will add to your sound. With your second finger at the second fret of the G string (third), play a downstroke. With the string vibrating, slide the second finger up to the fourth fret of the G string producing a B note. The string should still be ringing from the initial pick stroke. If not, repeat with slightly more pressure towards the fingerboard. The trick is to find the right amount of pressure that allows the string to keep ringing and is not too difficult to slide your finger.

▶ **EXERCISE THIRTEEN:**

This exercise combines all three left hand techniques.

▶ **EXERCISE FOURTEEN:**

11

Licks and Runs

"Licks" and "runs" are names for musical phrases that make up the vocabulary of flatpicking. Flatpickers love licks and runs, especially in the key of G. Here are some popular phrases. Be sure to follow the pick direction indicators.

▶ **EXERCISE FIFTEEN:**

Here are some in C.

▶ **EXERCISE SIXTEEN:**

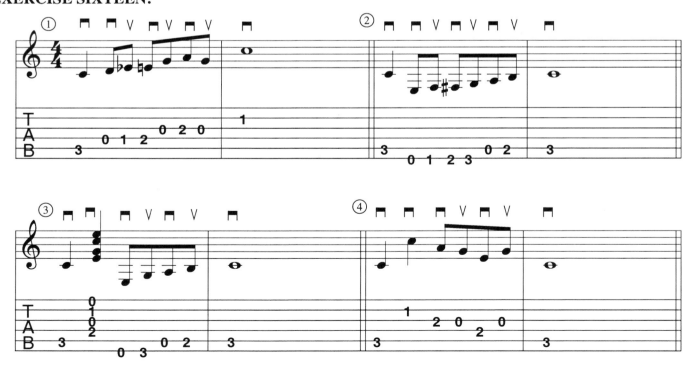

And in D

▶ **EXERCISE SEVENTEEN:**

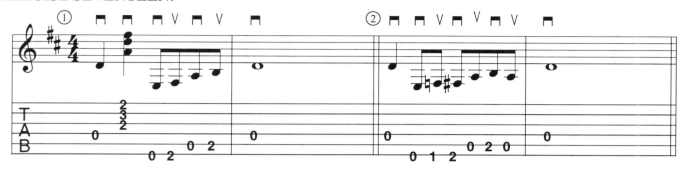

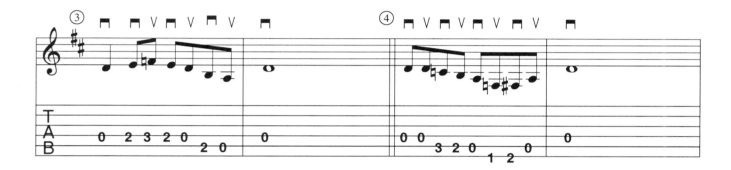

Try some licks with strums in this exercise

▶ **EXERCISE EIGHTEEN:**

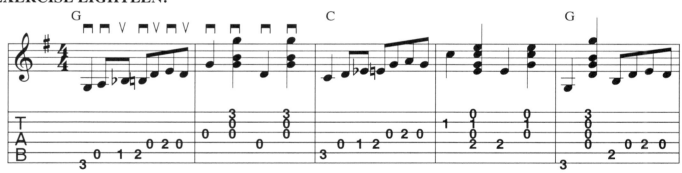

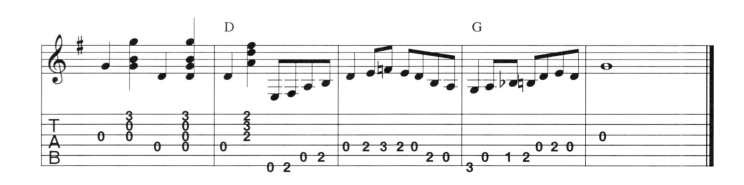

The Carter Style

Maybelle Carter was an early pioneer of American country music. As a member of the famous Carter Family, she recorded an incredible collection of country music from the late 1920s through the 1930s. As a guitarist, she left an even greater legacy . . . Carter style guitar.

Nearly every country guitarist knows at least one Carter style tune. It's simple beauty has made it a favorite of players and listeners for years. It is a great style for a lone guitarist because it provides both melody and rhythm. In this first tune, keep your fingers on the indicated chord as much as possible. Many of the melody notes are in the chords.

This classic guitar piece was originally recorded in G by Maybelle Carter in the early 1930s. Strive for a clean and buzz free sound.

► **EXERCISE NINETEEN:**

Wildwood Flower - Key of G

Playing in the key of C, we encounter an F chord. Fret only the first, second and third strings of the F chord for this arrangement. After you have learned these two versions, try playing them one after the other.

▶ **EXERCISE TWENTY:**

Wildwood Flower - Key of C

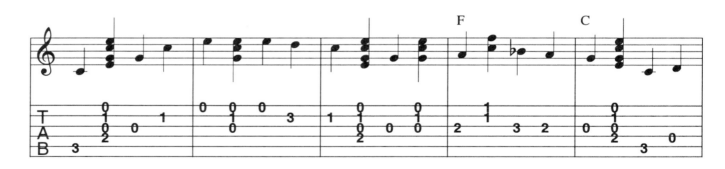

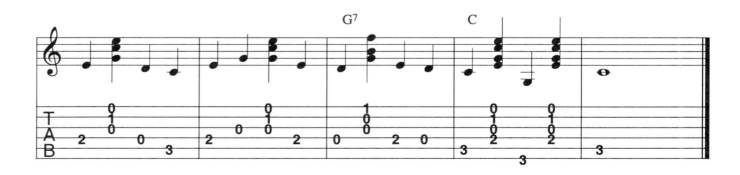

Flatpicking Fiddle Tunes

Players such as Jimmie Rodgers, Riley Puckett with the Skillet Lickers, Sam and Kirk Magee, and the Delmore Brothers were the early models of flatpicking. In the 1950s, musicians like Don Reno further developed the role of acoustic lead guitar in country music. For many people, Doc Watson was a mind-blowing introduction to the possibilities of fast, clean picking on the flattop guitar. In the 1960s, he and the legendary Clarence White made a place for guitar flatpicking in folk, bluegrass and country music. Soon players including Norman Blake, Dan Crary, and Tony Rice were pushing the boundaries and increasing the popularity of flatpick style guitar. Today, David Grier, Steve Kaufman, Bryan Sutton and a host of others continue the development of this exciting style.

Doc Watson and the players who followed him used fiddle tunes as the basis of the flatpicking style. Fiddle tunes remain the core of the flatpicking repertoire. We'll start by learning a standard favorite. Play this version of "Old Joe Clark" using all downstrokes. Where there is a rest, keep counting, but don't play. To play this tune in the common fiddle key of A, place a capo at the second fret.

▶ **EXERCISE TWENTY-ONE:**

Old Joe Clark

All Downstrokes

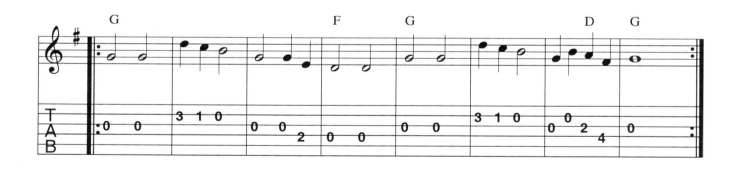

The following version adds some upstrokes to the arrangement. The mixture of quarter and eighth notes helps fill out the tune. Play slowly and pay close attention to pick direction.

► **EXERCISE TWENTY-TWO:**

Old Joe Clark II

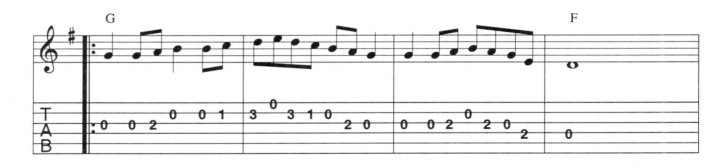

"Old Joe Clark III" features a fiddle-like melody using mostly eighth notes. While you are learning this version, stop at the end of each measure and check to see that the last note of the measure was played with a upstroke. If not, back track and find out where you are playing two consecutive downstrokes or upstrokes. This is likely to occur when the melody moves to a new string. Spend extra time here to get it right. It will pay off as you move through the rest of this book.

▶ **EXERCISE TWENTY-THREE:**

Old Joe Clark III

This is a popular American fiddle tune played here in the key of C. To play with a fiddler, put a capo at the second fret and it will come out in key of D, the common fiddle key for this song. Pay close attention to pick direction.

► **EXERCISE TWENTY-FOUR:**

Arkansas Traveler

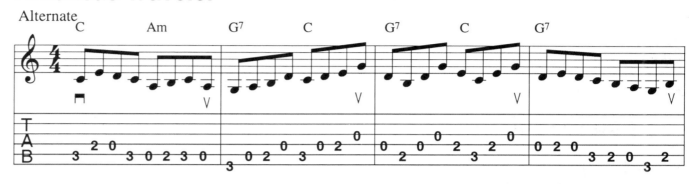

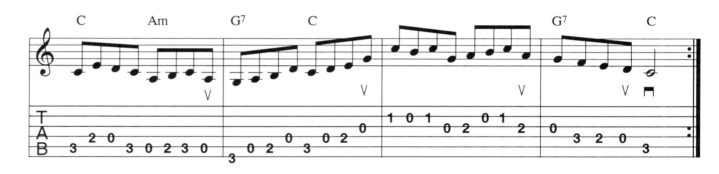

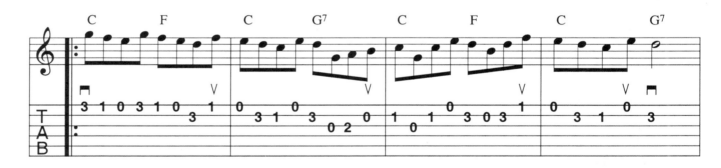

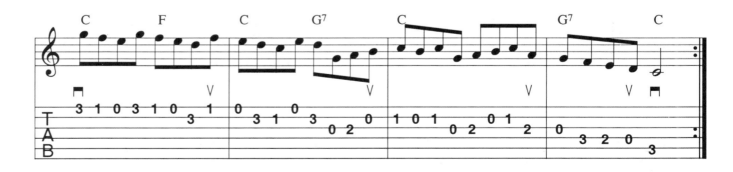

These are the first two tunes I have all my beginning students play. After they have learned these tunes, I carefully watch them play, stroke by stroke, to confirm they are alternating pick strokes correctly. Before moving on, make sure you have this basic idea working for you. Video cameras can be a tremendous help here.

The first tunes were purposely arranged with lots of eighth notes, to help you lock in alternating picking. Most arrangements of fiddle tunes for the guitar feature a variety of note lengths, but the picking rules remain the same: Down on the downbeats; up on the upbeats. If you plan to play with others, practice and learn the chords and rhythm to each new tune.

This jam session favorite is closely related to the Irish song "Little Beggar Man." Capo at the second fret to play in A, and watch the pick directions.

▶ **EXERCISE TWENTY-FIVE:**

Red Haired Boy

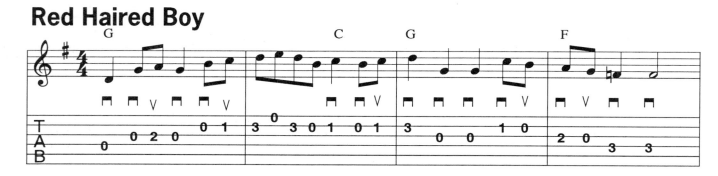

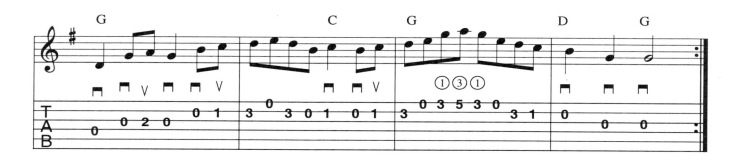

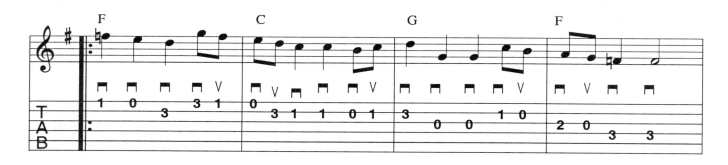

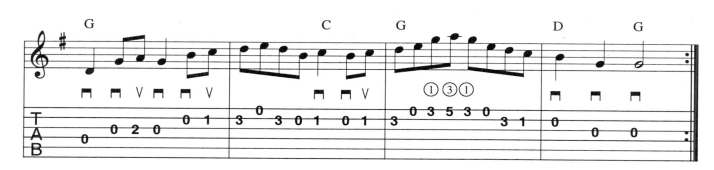

This popular tune is written in C position. Capo 2 for the more common key of D. The chords in parenthesis are optional. Listen to the rhythm both ways and decide for yourself.

▶ **EXERCISE TWENTY-SIX:**

Whiskey Before Breakfast

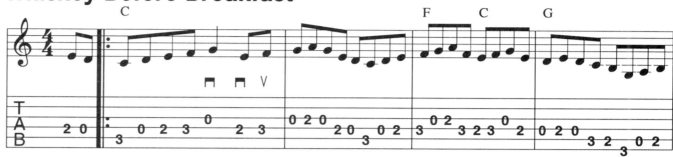

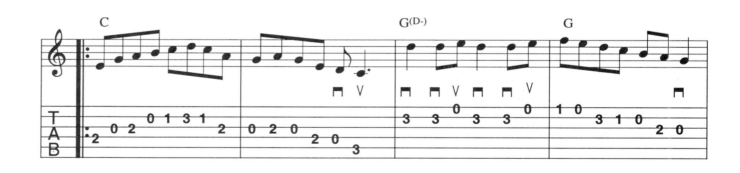

Developing Speed

By now, you have learned several flatpicking tunes and maybe you have tried to play them with other musicians. Sooner or later you will encounter people who play these tunes faster than you. Maybe everyone does! Here is a tested method for developing speed. It works for players of all levels. I still use it.

1. Memorize a tune so that you can play it without seeing the music. You may want to start with just an A or B section or a four measure phrase. If there are pauses in your performance of the tune while you are thinking of the next section, you don't have it memorized well enough. To play faster, you must know a tune really well.

2. Play the tune as you normally do, to get a sense of your comfortable speed.

3. Using a metronome or rhythm machine, find the tempo at which you are currently playing the tune. Be sure you can play cleanly with the click at this speed with no mistakes. Note the speed.

4. Reset the rhythm to a speed a little slower than your beginning speed. Example: if your beginning speed was 44 beats per minute (bpm), set the rhythm to 40 bpm.

5. Play the material several times with the beat until you have "settled in" to the tempo.

6. Advance the rhythm to the original tempo and play the material several times, listening for clean picking.

7. Advance to the next available increment on the machine and play, always listening for precision and clarity.

8. Repeat #7 until your playing is acceptable.

In a ten minute session, you will be able to advance several increments as you warm up. Write down this information. After a week or more of this work, you may be able to start at a higher speed. After several months, you may find you have increased your comfortable picking speed by ten or more bpm with the same clarity and control as when you began. Record your progress separately for each tune. Use this technique early in your practice sessions and only for ten minutes or so. Then move on to learning new songs or just picking for fun.

In addition to this incremental practice, you should spend some practice time trying to play at "real" tempos. Play along with recordings or set the rhythm machine to a fast speed. During this time, you are not striving for perfection. Your goal is to simply "keep up" with the music. If you drop individual notes or even entire phrases, wait momentarily and start back in when you can find a spot to enter. The plan here is to get you used to actual playing speeds, so you can perform with others now. You may find that by dropping a few notes from your arrangement, you are better able to keep up. This is a good method and your incremental practice will help you add back those notes in the future.

▶ EXERCISE TWENTY-SEVEN:

Basic Open Major Scales

Below are the major (do-re-mi) scales in open position for five common keys. Notice in C and G how the scales tones are the same notes that appear in the first fiddle tunes in this book. You needn't memorize this material at this time, but start being aware of the scales forms and the note names. If you haven't already, memorize the names of the open strings: E (6), A (5), D (4), G (3), B (2), E (1).

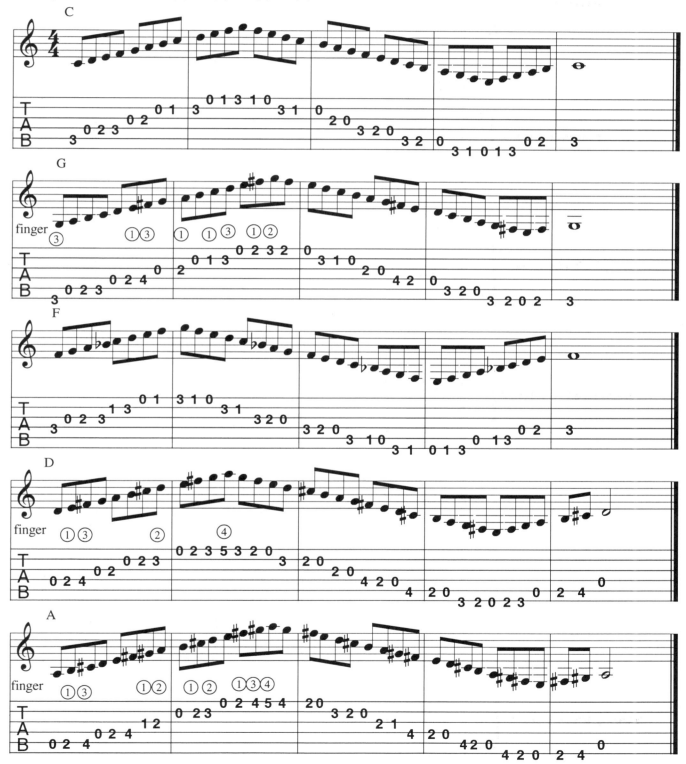

Fingerboard Note Chart

	SIXTH STRING	FIFTH STRING	FOURTH STRING	THIRD STRING	SECOND STRING	FIRST STRING
OPEN STRING NOTES	E	A	D	G	B	E
FIRST FRET	F	B♭ or A#	E♭ or D#	A♭ or G#	C	F
	F# or G♭	B	E	A	C# or D♭	F# or G♭
THIRD FRET	G	C	F	B♭ or A#	D	G
	A♭ or G#	C# or D♭	F# or G♭	B	E♭ or D#	A♭ or G#
FIFTH FRET	A	D	G	C	E	A
	B♭ or A#	E♭ or D#	A♭ or G#	C# or D♭	F	B♭ or A#
SEVENTH FRET	B	E	A	D	F# or G♭	B
	C	F	B♭ or A#	E♭ or D#	G	C
	C# or D♭	F# or G♭	B	E	A♭ or G#	C# or D♭
	D	G	C	F	A	D
	E♭ or D#	A♭ or G#	C# or D♭	F# or G♭	B♭ or A#	E♭ or D#
TWELFTH FRET	E	A	D	G	B	E

Chord Chart

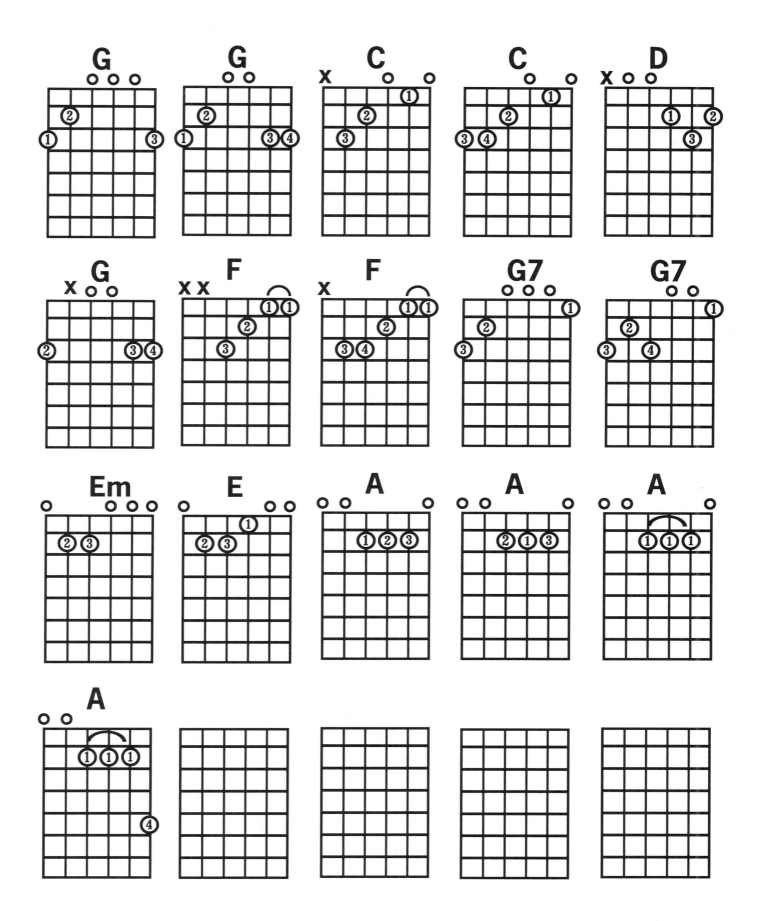

Fingering

Many beginning flatpickers think of home position on the guitar as first finger - first fret, second finger - second fret, etc. In the key of C, this is a natural position, but in other keys it presents problems. Here is a lick in G.

▶ **EXERCISE TWENTY-EIGHT:**

In the first finger/first fret position, this lick would be played with the second and fourth fingers. Try it. Now switch to the first and third fingers. Most players find this second option easier. Here are two fingerings for the open G scale.

▶ **EXERCISE TWENTY-NINE:**

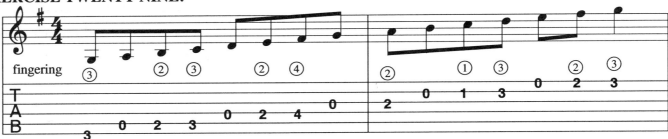

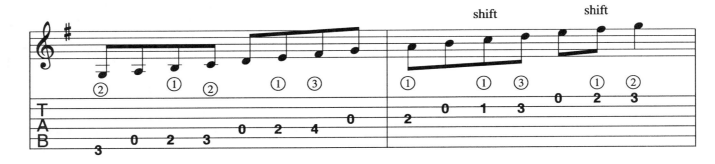

Generally, most open position flatpicking should be done in the first finger/second fret position. When you need notes in the first fret. Shift your hand so that you are in the first finger/first fret position. Professional players constantly shift between these two positions.

NOTE TO THE UNCONVINCED

   Some students feel that using the first finger/second fret position favors the 1, 2 and 3 fingers to the exclusion of the 4 finger. They feel they should be using the 4 finger more to build it up. In the open position this is true. The 1, 2, and 3 fingers will do most of the work. Even for experienced players, the 1-3 finger combination remains stronger than the 2-4 combination.

   When you begin to move up the neck and explore closed positions, the little finger becomes much more important. If you want to, by all means, practice playing open position fiddle tunes in the first finger/first fret position. Be aware, however, that in performance, most accomplished players shift between these two positions to optimize the use of their strongest fingers.

Syncopation

You should be comfortable now picking combinations of eighth and quarter notes. So far all the phrases have begun on the downbeat. Some of the following tunes contain syncopations or phrases that begin on the upbeat. The rules are the same in these situations. If a phrase begins on an "and" beat, start with an upstroke and continue normally. If the first note of the measure is an eighth note followed by a quarter (ex 30), play the eighth note down and the quarter up. The next note will be played with an up since the duration of the quarter note took up the "time" of the downstroke which would have occurred in the downbeat.

If this seems confusing right now, just play through the examples below paying close attention to the pick directions. With a little practice, these patterns will begin to "feel" right.

Here are examples of various rhythms and how to play them. Count the rhythms aloud until you get the rhythm.

▶ **EXERCISE THIRTY:**

Count out loud until you get the rhythm.

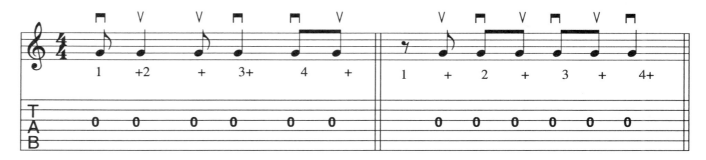

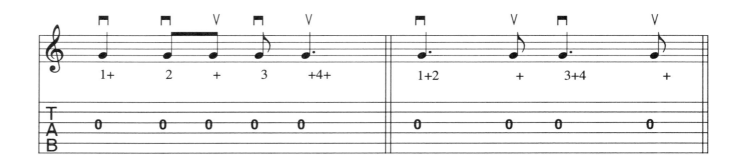

Notice what happens when a note is added or removed from this introduction lick.

► **EXERCISE THIRTY-ONE:**

Jam Session Favorites

Now you are ready to learn more fiddle tunes. The following tunes are popular at jam sessions. Remember to follow the pick direction rules.

► **EXERCISE THIRTY-TWO:**

Cripple Creek - Capo 2

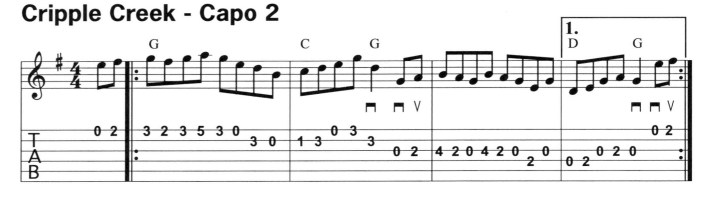

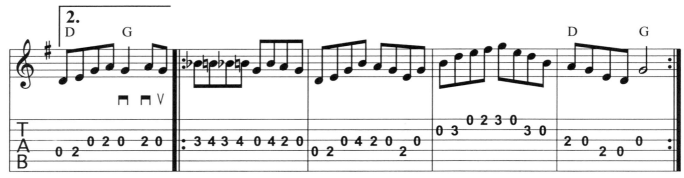

► **EXERCISE THIRTY-THREE:**
Temperance Reel

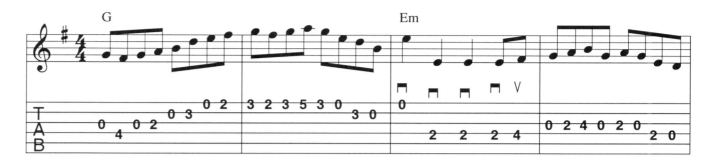

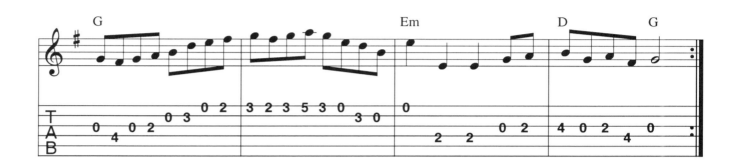

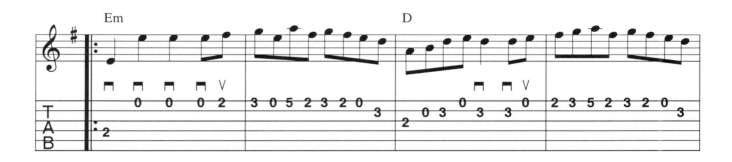

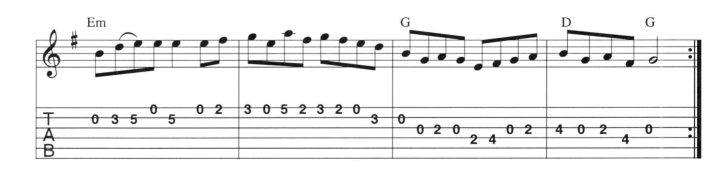

34

▶ **EXERCISE THIRTY-FOUR:**
Ragtime Annie

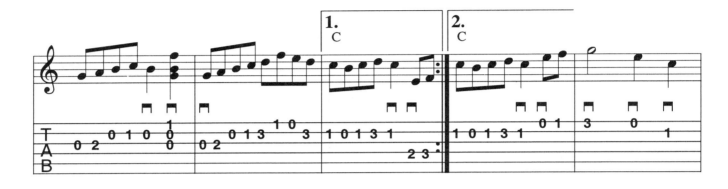

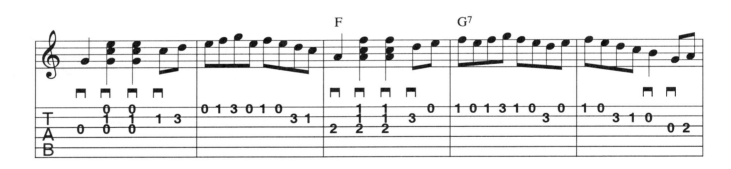

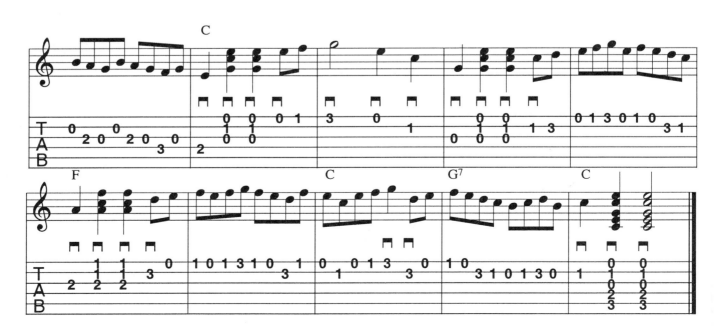

► **EXERCISE THIRTY-FIVE:**

Salt River (aka Salt Creek)

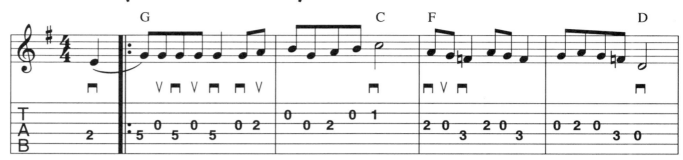

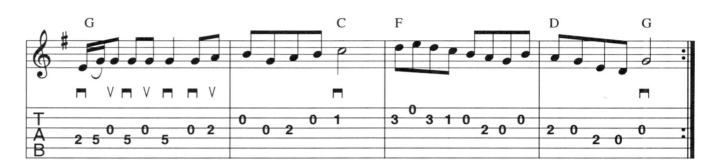

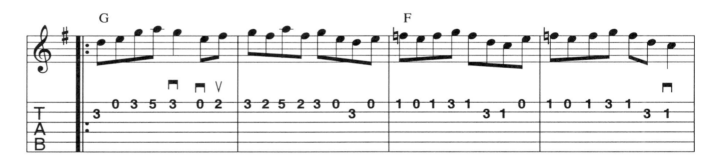

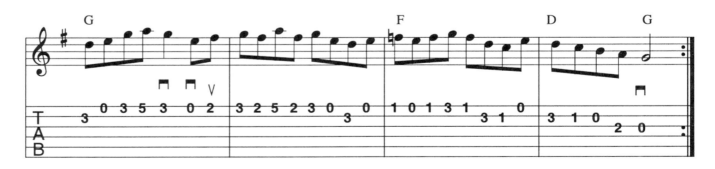

Playing Up the Neck

To prepare you to play up the neck, first learn the second position D scale. Use the first finger/second fret fingering and follow the indicated fingerings closely.

▶ **EXERCISE THIRTY-SIX:**

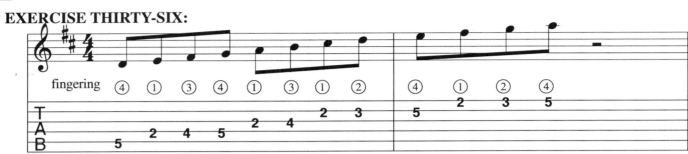

Try "Whiskey Before Breakfast" using the scale position we just learned.

▶ **EXERCISE THIRTY-SEVEN:**

Most players would not play "Whiskey" in this manner because it is fourth finger intensive and it lacks the open string sound associated with flatpicking. This arrangement in open D uses open strings where they are available. It results in a more characteristic sound and is more playable.

▶ **EXERCISE THIRTY-EIGHT:**

Whiskey Before Breakfast

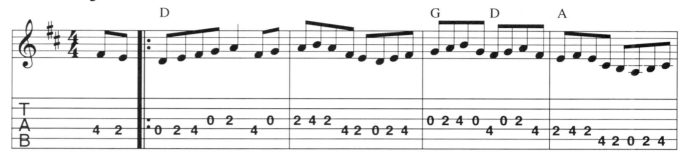

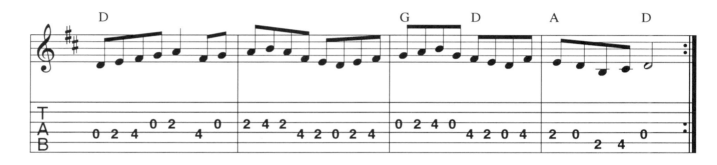

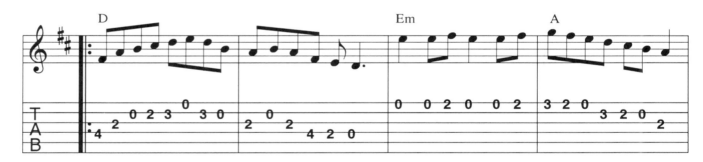

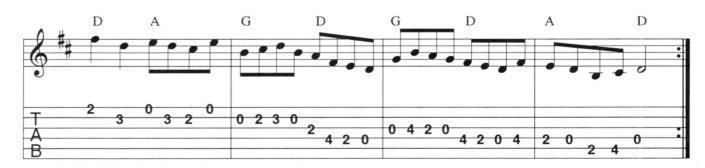

Second Position A Scale

Play this scale and try "Red Haired Boy" in this closed fingering.

**EXERCISE THIRTY-NINE:**

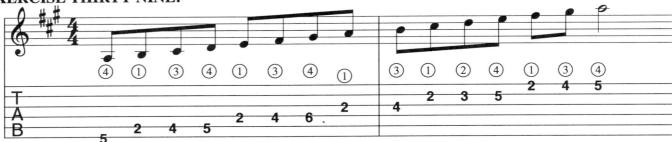

EXERCISE FORTY:

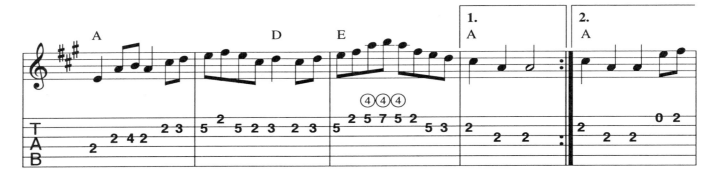

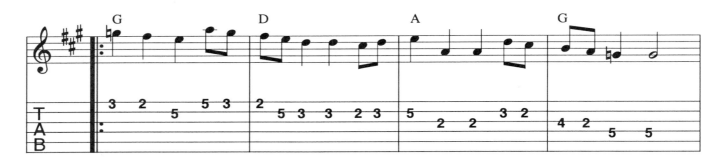

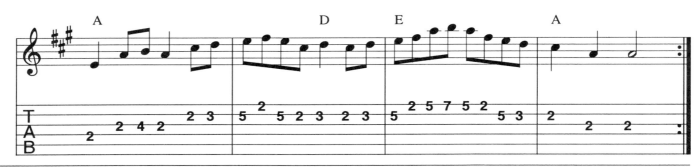

The difficult 4,4,4 fingering in the next to last measure is avoided in this next open string arrangement.

 41

▶ **EXERCISE FORTY-ONE:**
Red Haired Boy II

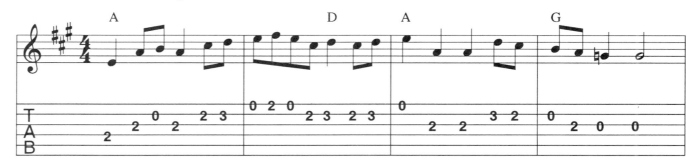

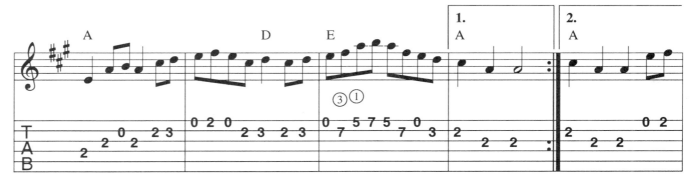

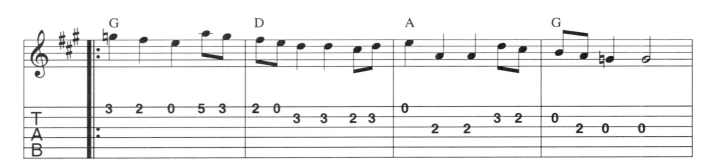

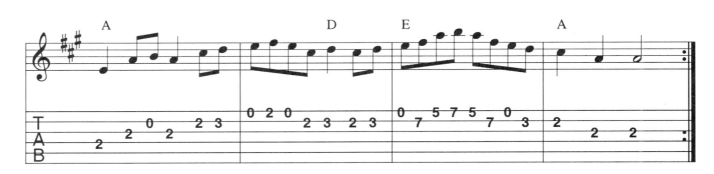

Crosspicking

Cross picking is an attractive flatpicking style that produces the sound of fingerpicking. The basic idea is a picking pattern played over three adjacent strings. Try this exercise using alternating picking.

► **EXERCISE FORTY-TWO:**

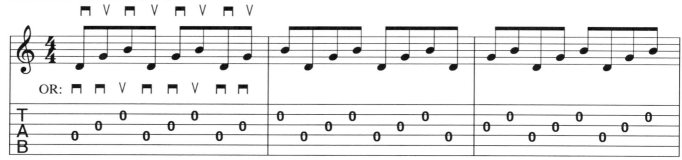

Try the same pattern holding a C chord.

► **EXERCISE FORTY-THREE:**

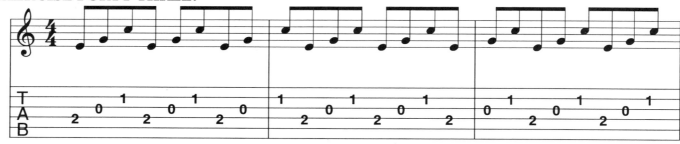

Now a D.

► **EXERCISE FORTY-FOUR:**

Now try all three together.

► **EXERCISE FORTY-FIVE:**

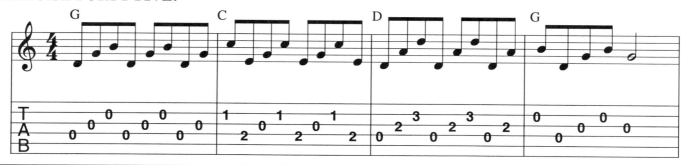

Some players prefer a special picking technique for crosspicking. Try playing the above exercises with two downstrokes followed by an upstroke. The pattern looks like: down, down, up, down, down, up. This is called a forward roll. A reverse roll can be played two ways as well. Either an alternating or an up, up, down, up, up, down pattern can be used. Try out both approaches in the following tunes. Only you can decide which pattern works best.

Here is Wildwood Flower arranged in the crosspicking style. Notice that to fill a measure, the pattern is two groups of three notes followed by two notes. Either alternate or play this pattern:
down, down, up, down, down, up, down, up.

► **EXERCISE FORTY-SIX:**
Wildwood Flower - Crosspicking
Forward Roll, down-down up or alternate

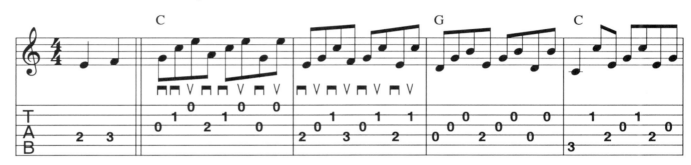

Reverse Roll

This arrangement combines crosspicking sections with straight picking. When the crosspicking phase is completed, return to regular alternating picking. If you crosspick this with alternating strokes, just continue as normal.

 EXERCISE FORTY-SEVEN:

Hand Me Down My Walking Cane

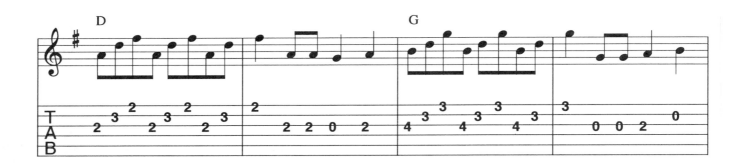

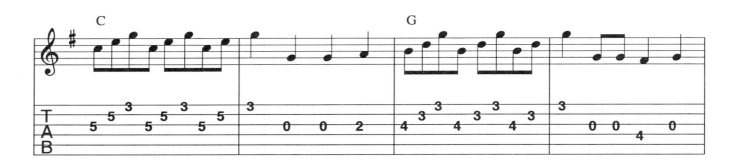

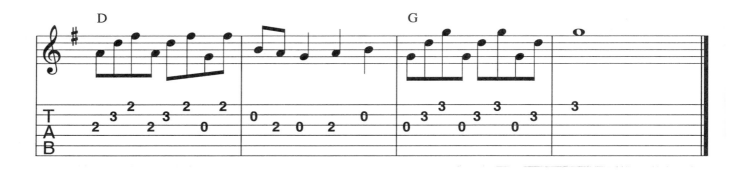

Advanced Arrangements

Here are two arrangements of popular jam tunes for your repertoire.

▶ **EXERCISE FORTY-EIGHT:**

Blackberry Blossom

Be careful with this one. In some parts of the country, they play the B section first and end with the A section.

▶ **EXERCISE FORTY-NINE:**

Bill Cheatham

Conclusion

I hope this book helps you on the road to becoming a good flatpicker. In over twenty years of teaching, I have encountered many beginner problems which I have been careful to cover in detail in these pages. Remember to play slowly and cleanly before you speed up. Fast and sloppy should not be one of your goals. If you have worked through all this material, you are ready for any of the flatpicking guitar fiddle tune anthologies currently on the market. If you are comfortable with reading standard notation, check out a fiddle tune collection. Just one of these books contains years of information.